RITES OF ALIENATION

RITES *of* ALIENATION

Douglas Fetherling

Quarry Press

The publisher thanks The Canada Council and the Ontario Arts Council for assistance in publishing this book.

CANADIAN CATALOGUING IN PUBLICATION DATA

Fetherling, Douglas, 1949–
Rites of Alienation

Poems.
ISBN 0-919627-94-3
1. Haiku, Canadian (English). I. Title.
PS8561.E834R48 1988 C811'.54 C88-090286-8
PR9199.3.F48 1988

for Vera Frenkel

The cover illustration is a detail from Figure *by Douglas Fetherling (oil on canvas, 1985).*
Design and imaging by ECW *Production Services, Sydenham, Ontario. Printed by Hignell Printing Limited, Winnipeg, Manitoba.*

Published by Quarry Press, Inc., P.O. Box 1061, Kingston, Ontario K7L 4Y5

Distributed by University of Toronto Press, 5201 Dufferin Street, Downsview, Ontario M3H 5T8

Dead street late at night
even the homeless gone home
a blind man's cane protruding from the garbage

Parking lot attendant
in lonely hut with saxophone
an audience of empty Buicks

Let the record show
that details are lacking —
bogus dawn hesitates over rooftops

Alms from heaven
night-birds strike the CN Tower
breakfast for the derelicts

The present is blocking the future
southbound towards delusion
seven a.m. on the Don Valley Parkway

Bits of old messages
in layers on the phone machine
a bristle from the brush embedded in the portrait

Old man sitting in the park
grey pullover keeps out autumn
the last leaf remaining on the tree

Two joggers in the rain
a red-haired woman reading Aldous Huxley
— not much to show for a day's work

Conscience and indigestion
danger increases as the seasons change
utopia made her claustrophobic

Petroglyphs sprayed in alleys
but invocations go unanswered
the innocent traveller steps from the kerb

Big greasy snowflakes
plunging to the street outside
the waitress 10 years older than she was 6 weeks ago

Tomorrow's archaeology today
the mirror's backed up again
office towers sweating

Main title theme & incidental music
the waitress is really an actress
tips & applause

The walls inhale
thinking of Byzantium
seven passengers arise

He answered the door once too often
got nailed
three days later resurrection

Through broken plant windows
rusty railyard, cold lake empty
view from the Bathurst Street bridge

"The city is something you do with space" (Thos Merton)
buildings bend before they break
sway in time with the silence

The world is too much with us
we have given our hearts away
says the man taking notes at the party

Language derives from sighs
bills of atonement
the past is legally binding

Buzzards stake out those
who circle in four-door sedans;
two weeks of expressionist rain

The after-hours joint
where the bartenders all hang out
the animals' field-trip to the zoo

Quiet the streetcars sleep here
fresh snow a security device
predators trapped in deafness

Young company with
enormous growth potential
needs your bones for fertilizer

Benefits & profit sharing
bright future for right person
bright future for wrong reasons

Ideal applicant will be
a self starter
should have begun by now

Old wallpaper
down down, layer after layer
each one nearer the truth

Rain will wash away
what the windows have seen —
the image heals itself

Language has been compromised
the evidence points to us
we reinvent ourselves once more

Memory lapses, distortion, evasion
nobody knows who first owned it
their lifestory grew like a folksong

The heart's a cave where feeling lurks
the figure hatched from the stone
the river overflows its banks

Blackmail often found in nature
the wind goes unreported
snows muffle

A crooked face in the mirror
rewrites itself—
truth concave, never convex

Undocumented language
impossible to trace it
the less said now the better

Return journeys always lighter
we choke on tears
leaving stains instead of shadows

Nightwear nightware nightmare nightmirror
we're locked in these conspiracies together
a kind of black communion

The hare pulls back from the wolf
horizon receding as we approach it
ambush a possibility

Nightshade nightshape nightweight nightscrape
rust the strongest bond all right
but which is the strictest emotion?

Neither proof nor cover-up
conspirators can be victims
not implicated in anybody's dreams

Memories command a premium
the transcript proves it
but I digress

The night continues to expand —
somewhere dogs ask questions
for sirens to answer

Are we rushing or escaping?
elderly nomenclature
does not keep the hunter humble

Master does well to emulate dog
stop breathing every few seconds
listen hard for enemies

Too many secrets swallowed dry
new shoes squeak underfoot
branches moan in the wind aloft

Three men wearing silhouettes
hazy figures on a railway trestle
my lawyer advises me to write no more today

The moon swings
in an east to west arc
three shots for a dollar win a prize

Wind in tall spruce
covers the sound
of the river

The land is mostly water
the contest lasts for eons
floods keep score

Trust the road to remain beneath us
reckless in blue-black night
frantic for a destination

Salvation
light in farmhouse window
like warm yellow cheese

The clouds withdraw
dragging their wounded shadows
across the field to safety

An arrow to indicate the Fraser
thin line of buildings
near the canyon floor

Brand new moon! improved!
expensive stars on violet background
skies advertise the heavens

The continent ends in exhaustion
timid waves a form of welcome
you coin the term British Columbia

The ocean snores and wheezes
hands of the clock like an insect's feelers
desperately seeking the past

People at the aeroport
dragging bags pets children
only the bags are on wheels

Spring is our manumission
perfection we rejoice in
then the cat eats a butterfly

Staring the way a lip-reader does
at the jukebox of dreams
unable to decide

To live longer is to concentrate
on speed devoid of motion;
wait for riders passing by

Who picks the ending supplies the meaning
words in clusters not regular breaths
conversation has ceased being oral

The prisoner ties blankets together
like St John of the Cross (or Jimmy Cagney)
ivy up the barbed wire creeps

The flame stumbles then rights itself
with opening and closing of the door
deliveries : departures

Tears from beneath the blindfold
just think about them and snap they're gone
the blindfold is a kindness really

Everything was obvious in context
a bottle of blended
a distinguished air

Knocking at the gate in code
speaking fluent gibberish
less civilisation than is called for

Faint carbon paper tattoo
image slips away like a dream
objects leaving unclaimed stories behind

Entire new season of desires
hidden among the effects
countervailing shadows

Starting a new list
rescue paraphernalia
untranslatable scrawls

Retroactive silence
the saxophone expunged
our feet create erasures

The night falters
moving towards repose
harmony with a bit of kick

Second class citizens
second class train
second class surprise

Shadows crosshatched
dark to light
the sun erases

Inviting confusion
the ratio of dead to living
plugs began falling from their sockets

Our faults do not redeem us
we're disposed of when we're gone
lightbulb no substitute for fire

In wind or underwater makes no difference
elements are there to grind us down
the I of the poem, the you of the song

Read on
ransacking shelves
the dead leave messages in books

The moon's brown nipples —
every object in the room
emitting a metallic buzz

Positive ID
tattoos shaped like stains
appear then disappear

Progress towards decay
it just got away from us somehow
the city sprung

Unwelcome reminders of the dead
not facts you can look up
astringent though the wound healed long ago

Bad storm brewing
neatly xeroxed leaves
torn from the trees

Height precedes width
etiquette demands it
organic forces exerting control

Branches thick on the ground
nostalgia for the storm absolute
reminiscent thunder

We vary our routine
the enemy are reptiles
never wear the same skin twice

Hermit with no hermitage
stands firm on paradox
a name is still required

Art flourishes in strange precincts
life classes offered at the morgue
books written at the university

Not the poet but her poem
not the image but the sight
the process lived, not the act observed

One cannot rest
in one's own shadow —
seek the shade of friends

Self-educated
never had a lesson in our lives
no one to share the blame

Old movies:
the dead cavort on screen
the reel unwinds

The rain searches everywhere
we hold our breath
act nonchalant

Disappeared
while on retreat
lapsed into exile like a coma

High notes piercing the wall —
visible through the window
a plastic moon with cigarette burns

What's left nourishes
make sure it's someone else's
we misjudge our own nostalgia

We know at all times where our shadows are
but are we inconspicuous
in the desert?

Self-destruction
if you want it done right
do it yourself

A little place in Zen Street
buttons on the mattress, life goes on
the blood has settled in the roof of your mouth

In hot countries near the floor
we stand erect as bad air rises
jaywalking a western crime

The future is forewarned
lying heavily upon the shelves
a trace of history around the rim

Typhoon forecast
wisteria
hysterical

88 keys
37 buddhas
14 names for despair